Ashes to Alleluia

An Offering of Lenten Reflections

AMY LAUREN MILLER

Published by Whistling Girl Press, Collierville, TN
First Edition Paperback, 2026
Library of Congress Control Number: 2026901087
ISBN: 979-8-218-91487-5
amylaurenmiller.com

A Note from the Author

This earnest labor of love was born out of a desire for a Lenten practice at a time in my life when everything seemed hard and God seemed far away. Desiring to strengthen my faltering faith, I was determined to do *something*, but I was very much afraid of failure.

So I decided to write a poem everyday and post it on my social media pages as a way to hold myself accountable. Still, I was a little intimidated. Could I find something to write about *every* day of Lent? Remaining uncertain, I settled on the shortest form of poetry familiar to me – the Haiku. What came of this daily practice was a drilled down, back to basics, essentials only set of poems that seemed to resonate with many of my readers. I hope it speaks to you in a meaningful and unencumbered way and that it blesses your journey through Lent.
Each haiku is paired with a scripture for further reflection.

May you experience a deeper connection to our Savior, as well as discernment in your journey to the foot of the cross.
May you know for certain that, even when we do not feel a sense of closeness to our Creator, that *His* faithfulness meets us wherever we are.
May you know deep in your being what Julian of Norwich so beautifully wrote:

All shall be well, and all shall be well, and all manner of things shall be well, for there is a force of love moving through the universe that holds us fast and will never let us go.

To God be all glory and honor!

1

THE JOURNEY BEGINS
WITH ASHES ON MY FOREHEAD
SURRENDERING SELF

So I turned to the Lord God and pleaded with him in prayer and petition, in fasting, and in sackcloth and ashes.

Daniel 9:3

2

IN THE WILDERNESS
OF MY SELF IMPOSED EXILE
HE MEETS ME THERE

See, I am doing a new thing! Now it springs up; do you not percieve it? I am making a way in the wilderness and streams in the wasteland.

Isaiah 44:3

3

AS I TURN INWARD
HIS PEACE QUIETS THE CHAOS
HE RESTORES MY SOUL

The Lord is my shepherd, I lack nothing. He makes me lie down in green pastures, he leads me beside quiet waters, he refreshes my soul. He guides me along the right paths for his name's sake.

Psalm 23:1-3

4

IN THIS SACRED TIME
TAKING REST IN REFLECTION
HE TENDS MY SOUL

The Lord is close to the brokenhearted and saves those who are crushed in spirit.

Psalm 34:18

5

SILENT SOLITUDE
THOUGHTS BECOMING AWARENESS
MY SINS ARE CONFESSED

Whoever conceals their sins does not prosper, but the one who confesses and renounces them finds mercy.

Proverbs 28:13

6

PRODIGAL DAUGHTER
WEARING THE SMUDGE OF MY SIN
STILL HE WELCOMES ME

But if we walk in the light, as he is in the light, we have fellowship with one another, and the blood of Jesus, his son, purifies us from all sin.

I John 1:7

7

WORLD WEARY AND WORN
IN BODY, MIND AND SPIRIT
HE OFFERS REFUGE

God is our refuge and strength, an ever present help in trouble.

Psalm 46:1

8

I REST AND WRESTLE
SEARCHING FOR MY LOST PIECES
HE FILLS EVERY VOID

Truly my soul finds rest in God; my salvation comes from him.

Psalm 62:1

9

THOUGH I SEEK HIS PEACE
I STILL GET LOST IN THE NOISE
THE WORLD IS SO LOUD

I have told you these things, so that in me you may have peace.
In this world you will have trouble. But take heart!
I have overcome the world.

John 16:33

10

BUT AS HE WHISPERS
QUIETING MY ANXIOUS THOUGHTS
I LEARN TO LET GO

Cast all your anxiety on him because he cares for you.

I Peter 5:7

11

RELEASING MY FEAR
HE FILLS ME WITH HIS COURAGE
AGAIN AND AGAIN

For the spirit God gave us does not make us timid,
but gives us power, love and self discipline.

II Timothy 1:7

12

DO NOT BE ANXIOUS
REMINDING MYSELF AGAIN
DO NOT BE ANXIOUS

So do not fear, for I am with you; do not be dismayed, for I am your God. I will strengthen you and help you. I will uphold you with my righteous right hand.

Isaiah 41:10

13

THE CHOICE BEFORE ME
SELF RELIANCE OR HIS WAY
THE STRUGGLE REMAINS

Trust in the Lord with all your heart and lean not on your own understanding; in all your ways submit to him, and he will make your paths straight.

Psalm 3:5-6

14

RELEARNING EACH DAY
ONE STEP FORWARD ONE GLANCE BACK
ONE PRAYER AT A TIME

Rend your hearts and not your garments.
Return to the Lord your God, for he is gracious and
compassionate, slow to anger and abounding in love, and
he relents from sending calamity.

Joel 2:13

15

I KEEP TAKING BACK
THE BURDENS HE HAS LIFTED
FORGETTING HIS GRACE

Come to me all you who are weary and burdened, and I will give you rest. Take my yoke upon you and learn from me, for I am gentle and humble in heart, and you will find rest for your souls. For my yoke is easy and my burden is light.

Matthew 11:28-30

16

TURNING TO HIS WORD
CHOOSING TO BELIEVE TODAY
KNOWING HE IS GOOD

*And we know that in all things God works for the good of
those who love him,
who have been called according to his purpose.*

Romans 8:28

17

RETURNING TO TRUTH
PRACTICING A CHILDLIKE FAITH
CLAIMING IT MY OWN

Truly, I tell you anyone who will not receive the kingdom of God like a little child will never enter it.

Mark 10:15

18

SING PRAISES TO HIM

LET MY REQUESTS BE MADE KNOWN

PRAY WITH THANKSGIVING

*Do not be anxious about anything, but in every situation, by
prayer and petition, with thanksgiving,
present your requests to God.
And the peace of God, which transcends all understanding,
will guard your hearts and your minds in Christ Jesus.*

Philippians 4:6-7

19

GRATITUDE IS JOY
REMEMBER HIS FAITHFULNESS
JOY IS GRATITUDE

Give thanks to the Lord, for he is good;
his love endures forever.

Psalm 118:1

20

EVEN IN SORROW
SURROUNDED BY THE WORLD'S PAIN
HE IS THERE WITH ME

Blessed are those who mourn for they will be comforted.

Matthew 5:4

21

WHAT DOES HE REQUIRE OF ME
ACT JUSTLY AND LOVE MERCY
WALK HUMBLY WITH HIM

He has shown you, O mortal, what is good.
And what does the Lord require of you?
To act justly and to love mercy, and to walk humbly with
your God.

Micah 6:8

22

DO NOT JUDGE OTHERS
LOVE MY NEIGHBOR AS MYSELF
PROCLAIM HIS GOODNESS

Jesus replied: "Love the Lord your God with all your heart, and with all your soul, and with all your mind. This is the first and greatest commandment. And the second is like it: 'Love your neighbor as yourself.'

Matthew 22:37-39

23

BE HIS HANDS AND FEET
SWIMMING AGAINST THE CURRENT
FOLLOWING HIS LEAD

For I was hungry and you gave me something to eat, I was thirsty and you gave me something to drink, I was a stranger and you invited me in, I needed clothes and you clothed me, I was sick and you looked after me, I was in prison and you came to visit me.

Matthew 25:35-40

24

IN DOING HIS WORK
I BECOME MORE THAN MYSELF
MISSIONAL MYSTERY

But you will receive power when the Holy Spirit comes on you, and you will be my witnesses in Jerusalem, and in all Judea and Samaria, and to the ends of the Earth.

Acts 1:8

25

DECIDING TO RISK
EXTRAVAGANT LOVE AND GRACE
FALLING ON MY KNEES

But God demonstrates his own love for us in this:
While we were still sinners, Christ died for us.

Romans 5:8

26

LEARNING TO ACCEPT
THE FULLNESS OF HIS MERCY
FORGIVING MYSELF

Let us then approach God's throne of grace with confidence, so that we may receive mercy and find grace to help us in our time of need.

Hebrews 4:16

27

SHEDDING THE DECEIT
OF SATAN'S PERSISTENT DOUBT
REFUSING THE LIE

Put on the full armor of God, so that you can take your stand against the devil's schemes.

Ephesians 6:11

28

NEEDING REMINDERS
TO SHIFT MY FOCUS ON HIM
BREATHING PRAYERS OF TRUST

*When I am afraid, I put my trust in you. In God, whose word
I praise - in God I trust, and am not afraid.
What can mere mortals do to me?*

Psalm 56:3-4

29

CONFESSING MY SHAME
HE DOES NOT AMPLIFY IT
BUT WASHES ME CLEAN

If we confess our sins, he is faithful and just and will forgive us our sins and purify us from all unrighteousness.

I John 1:9

30

ACCEPTING HIS WILL
LEARNING TO LOVE AS HE LOVES
SEEING CHRIST IN ALL

A new command I give you: Love one another.
As I have loved you, so you must love one another.
By this everyone will know that you are my disciples if you
love one another.

John 13:34-35

31

RELEARNING HIS GRACE
SUFFICIENT FOR MY SOJOURN
ENOUGH FOR THE DAY

But he said to me, my grace is sufficient for you, for my power is made perfect in weakness.
Therefore, I will boast all the more gladly about my weaknesses, so that Christ's power may rest on me.

II Corinthians 12:9

32

WHEN I UNRAVEL
HE KNITS ME BACK TOGETHER
UNTIL I AM WHOLE

May God himself, the God of peace, sanctify you through and through. May your whole spirit, soul and body be kept blameless at the coming of our Lord Jesus Christ. The one who calls you is faithful, and he will do it.

I Thessalonians 5:23-24

33

I DON'T NEED TO PROVE
THAT I'M WORTHY OF HIS LOVE
I'M HIS CREATION

*For it is by grace you have been saved through faith -
and this is not from yourselves, it is the gift of God -
not by works, so that no one can boast.*

Ephesians 2:8-9

34

I AM HIS GOOD WORK
THAT WHICH HE BEGAN IN ME
HE WILL MAKE COMPLETE

*In all my prayers, for all of you, I always pray with joy
because of your partnership in the gospel
from the first day until now,
being confident of this, that he who began a good work in
you will carry it on to completion
until the day of Christ Jesus.*

Philippians 1:4-6

35

AS A CHILD OF GOD
HE CALLS ME HIS BELOVED
HE WALKS BESIDE ME

You hem me in behind and before,
and you lay your hand upon me.

Psalm 139:5

36

COMFORT FELLOWSHIP
THE CONSOLATIONS OF CHRIST
COMPASSION AND LOVE

*Therefore, if you have any encouragement from being
united with Christ, if any comfort from his love, if any
common sharing in the Spirit, if any tenderness and
compassion, then make my joy complete by
being like-minded, having the same love, being one in spirit,
and of one mind.*

Philippians 2:1-2

37

GIFTS FOR THE JOURNEY
AS I BECOME MORE COMPLETE
BY HIS SAVING GRACE

*For in Christ all the fullness of the Deity lives in bodily form,
and in Christ you have been brought to fullness.
He is the head over every power and authority.*

Colossians 2:9-10

38

EVEN WITHOUT WORDS
HE HEARS THE CRIES OF MY HEART
THE DEEPEST PLEAS KNOWN

In the same way, the Spirit helps us in our weakness. We do not know what we ought to pray for, but the Spirit himself intercedes for us through wordless groans. And he who searches our hearts, knows the mind of the Spirit, because the Spirit intercedes for God's people in accordance with the will of God.

Romans 8:26-27

39

I TURN TO SCRIPTURE
HE WRITES HIS WORDS ON MY HEART
FOR THE DAYS AHEAD

This is the covenant I will establish with the people of Israel
after that time, declares the Lord.
I will put my laws in their minds
and write them on their hearts.
I will be their God, and they will be my people.

Hebrews 8:10

40
PALM SUNDAY

JERUSALEM WAITS
HIS LAST WEEK OF EARTHLY LIFE
THE PASSION OF CHRIST

A JOYFUL ENTRANCE
PALM BRANCHES STREWN ON THE GROUND
SHOUTS OF HOSANNAH

The next day, the great crowd that had come for the festival heard that Jesus was on his way to Jerusalem. They took palm branches and went out to meet him. shouting, "Hosanna!"
"Blessed is he who comes in the name of the Lord!"
"Blessed is the king of Israel!"

John 12:12-13

41

WITH EACH STEP FORWARD
THE WORK OF RECLAMATION
INSISTS ON THE TRUTH

*Create in me a pure heart, O God,
and renew a steadfast spirit within me.*

Psalm 51:10

42

WOULD I HAVE FOLLOWED
OR WOULD I HAVE DENIED HIM
THE QUESTIONS REMAIN

Peter replied, "Man, I don't know what you're talking about!"
Just as he was speaking, the rooster crowed. The Lord
turned and looked straight at Peter. Then Peter
remembered the word the Lord has spoken to him:
"Before the rooster crows today,
you will disown me three times."
And he went outside and wept bitterly.

Luke 22:60-62

43

ACCEPTING MY DOUBT
AS PART OF MY HUMAN WALK
HELP MY UNBELIEF

"If you can?" said Jesus.
"Everything is possible for one who believes."
Immediately the boy's father exclaimed,
"I do believe; help me overcome my unbelief!"

Mark 9:23-24

44
MAUNDY THURSDAY

THE PASSOVER MEAL
THIRTY PIECES OF SILVER
BETRAYED BY A FRIEND

THEY ARRESTED HIM
WHILE PRAYING IN THE GARDEN
HIS FRIENDS FELL ASLEEP

Returning the third time, he said to them,
"Are you still sleeping and resting? Enough! The hour has
come. Look, the Son of Man is delivered into the hands of
sinners. Rise! Let us go! Here comes my betrayer!"

Mark 14:41-42

45
GOOD FRIDAY

THREE CROSSES STANDING
HIS SPIRIT GOES OUT OF HIM
THE CURTAIN IS RENT

THEY BROKE HIS BODY
AND CAST LOTS FOR HIS CLOTHING
WHILE HE DIED FOR ME

When he had received the drink, Jesus said,
"It is finished."
With that, he bowed his head and gave up his spirit.

John 19:30

46

TAKING ON MY SIN
BEARING THE BURDEN FOR ALL
SACRIFICIAL LAMB

The next day, John saw Jesus coming toward him, and said,
"Look the Lamb of God,
who takes away the sins of the world!"

John 1:29

47

EASTER SUNDAY

HE IS RAISED FROM THE GRAVE

THE STONE HAS BEEN ROLLED AWAY

DEATH WHERE IS YOUR STING

HE'S RISEN INDEED

THE DAY OF RESURRECTION

SING ALLELUIA

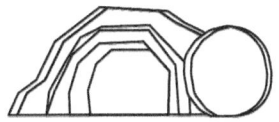

Where, O death, is your victory?
Where, O death, is your sting?
The sting of death is sin, and the power of sin is the law.
But thanks be to God!
He gives us the victory through our Lord Jesus Christ.

I Corinthians 15:55-57

Acknowledgements

Much love and gratitude to:

Michelle M. Hulett and Chuck for their eagle eye proofreading;
Richard Paul Evans' Author Ready for their guidance, support and community;
The Bunkhouse Book Tour authors for spurring me on;
everyone who dropped a like or a comment;
and most of all to:
Chuck and Miller for their unparalleled love, support and encouragement and
for believing in me before I believed in myself.

About the Author

Amy Lauren Miller began creating poetry and song lyrics from a very young age. Building on this natural form of self-expression, she has used her affinity for writing as an outlet for myriad observations and interests.

After a career in College Admission Counseling and a 15-year hiatus to stay home while raising her son, she is grateful for the opportunity to share her work on a larger scale. In addition to spiritual topics, Lauren writes stories for children which highlight overcoming challenges and celebrating our distinctive (and sometimes quirky) characteristics.

Her poems and essays are inspired by nature and life experiences. Much of her writing centers mainly on love or the disruption of it.

Lauren is married to her patiently steadfast husband and is blessed to be mother to their inspiring son. Together they have built their life in West Tennessee with two loyal, goofy dogs and one unruly, domineering cat.

She is also the author of the award winning children's book,
Blue Bruce the Christmas Spruce
(a collaboration with Memphis, Tennessee based artist Maggie Russell).

Amy Lauren Miller
WEAVER OF WORDS

amylaurenmiller.com

www.ingramcontent.com/pod-product-compliance
Lightning Source LLC
Chambersburg PA
CBHW020424130626
46549CB00006B/2730